CW01302157

Contents

Instructions

Each pair of cards are given a matching code.
A 'question card' will be on a facing page while each 'answer card' will be on the reverse side.

For example:
mp (M-04) is on a facing page.
To see the definition (Mezzo Piano – Medium Soft) turn over the same page.
It will also have M-04 in the bottom right corner.

All cards are landscape.

Topic	Card	Code	Page
Dynamics	Pianississimo	M-01	5
	Pianissimo	M-02	7
	Piano	M-03	9
	Mezzo-piano	M-04	11
	Mezzo-forte	M-05	13
	Forte	M-06	15
	Fortissimo	M-07	17
	Fortississimo	M-08	19
	Crescendo (symbol)	M-09	21
	Crescendo (abb)	M-10	23
	Decrescendo (symbol)	M-11	25
	Decrescendo (abb)	M-12	27
	Diminuendo (abb)	M-13	29
	Sforzando (abb)	M-14	31
Tempo	Larghissimo	N-01	33
	Grave	N-02	35
	Largo	N-03	37
	Lento	N-04	39
	Larghetto	N-05	41
	Adagio	N-06	43
	Adagietto	N-07	45
	Andante	N-08	47
	Andantino	N-09	49
	Marcia moderato	N-10	51
	Andante moderato	N-11	53
	Moderato	N-12	55
	Allegretto	N-13	57
	Allegro moderato	N-14	59
	Allegro	N-15	61
	Vivace	N-16	63
	Vivacissimo	N-17	65
	Allegrissimo	N-18	67
	Allegro vivace	N-19	69
	Presto	N-20	71
	Prestissimo	N-21	73
(other terms)	A piacere	0-01	75
	Con moto	0-02	77

	Assai	0-03	79
	A tempo	0-04	81
	L'istesso tempo	0-05	83
	Ma non tanto	0-06	85
	Ma non troppo	0-07	87
	Molto	0-08	89
	Poco	0-09	91
	Subito	0-10	93
	Tempo comodo	0-11	95
	Tempo di	0-12	97
	Tempo giusto	0-13	99
	Tempo semplice	0-14	101
	Tempo primo	0-15	103
(change in tempo)	Accelerando	P-01	105
	accel.	P-02	107
	Allargando	P-03	109
	Calando	P-04	111
	Doppio movimento	P-05	113
	Doppio piu lento	P-06	115
	Lentando	P-07	117
	Meno mosso	P-08	119
	Piu mosso	P-09	121
	Mosso	P-10	123
	Precipitando	P-11	125
	Rallentando	P-12	127
	rall.	P-13	129
	Ritardando	P-14	131
	rit.	P-15	133
	Ritenuto	P-16	135
	riten.	P-17	137
	Rubato	P-18	139
	Stretto	P-19	141
	Stringendo	P-20	143
	Tardando	P-21	145

M-01

Pianississimo
(Very very soft)

30 dB
(Quiet room)

M-01

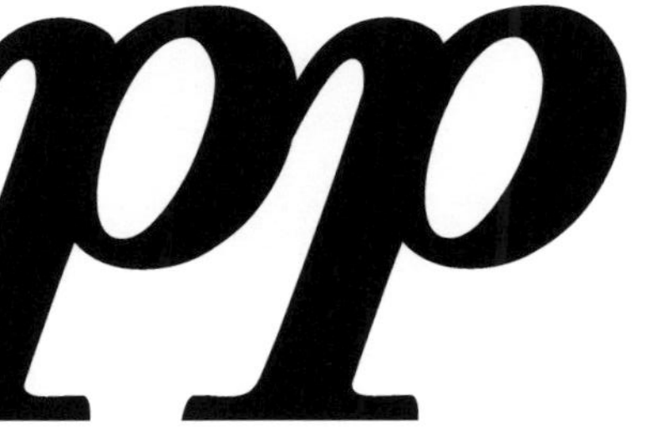

M-02

Pianissimo
(Very soft)

40 dB
(Moderate snoring)

M-02

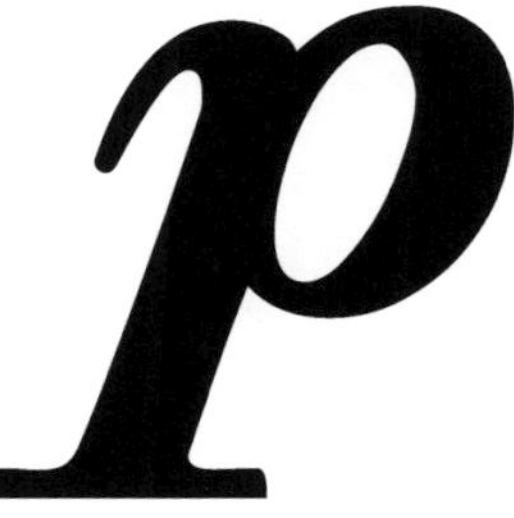

M-03

Piano
(Soft)

50 dB
(Conversation)

M-03

M-04

Mezzo Piano
(Medium soft)

60 dB
(Light traffic)

M-04

M-05

Mezzo Forte
(Medium loud)

70 dB
(Noisy restaurant)

M-05

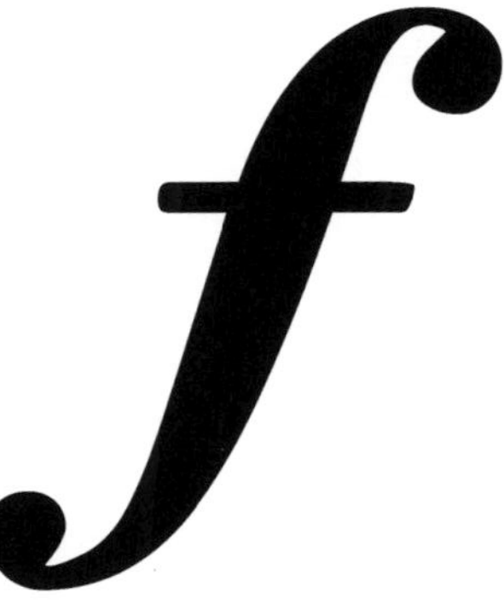

M-06

Forte
(Loud)

80 dB
(Busy traffic)

M-06

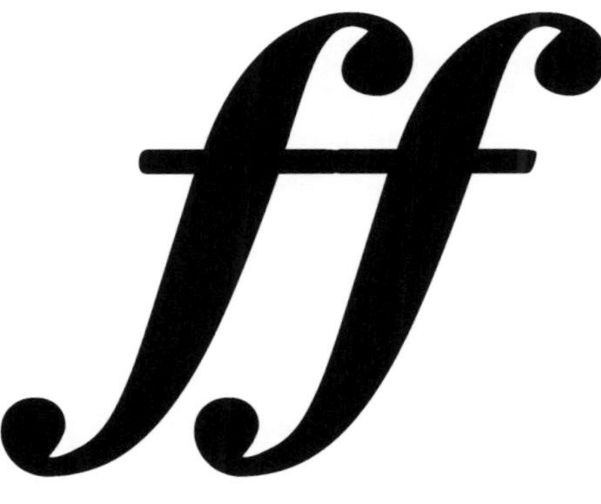

M-07

Fortissimo
(Very loud)

90 dB
(Lawnmower)

M-07

fff

Townsend Tuition

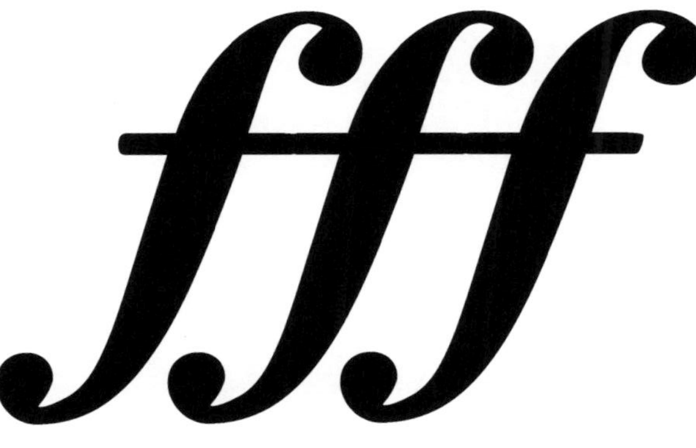

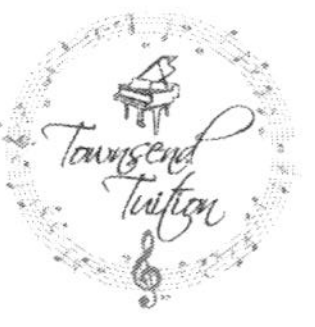

M-08

Fortississimo
(Very very loud)

100 dB
(Subway train)

M-08

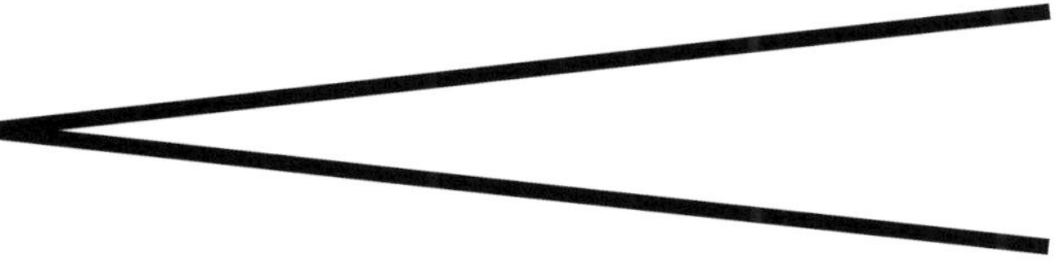

M-09

Crescendo

Gradual increase of loudness

M-09

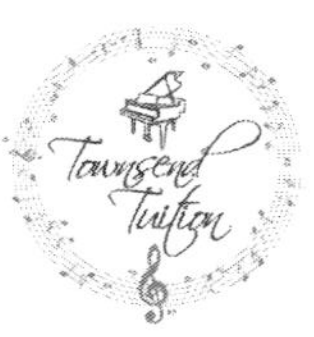
Townsend Tuition

cresc.

M-10

Crescendo

Gradual increase of loudness

M-10

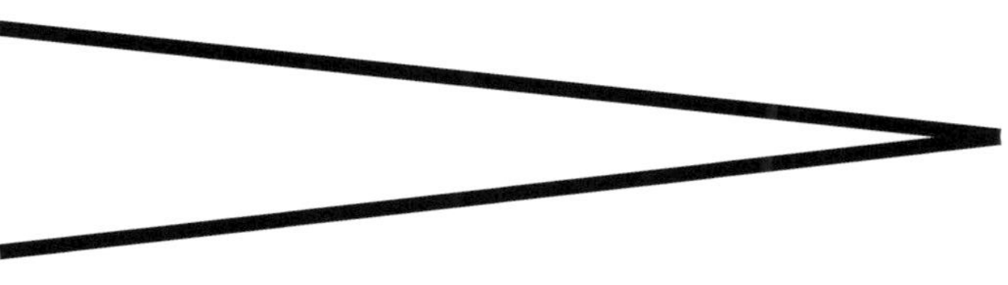

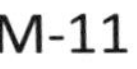

M-11

Decrescendo
(Diminuendo)

Gradual decrease of loudness

M-11

decresc.

M-12

Decrescendo

Gradual decrease of loudness

M-12

M-13

Diminuendo

Gradual decrease of loudness

M-13

M-14

Sforzando

Forced accent

M-14

Larghissimo

N-01

As slow as possible

(24 bpm and under)

N-01

Grave

N-02

Very slow (and solemn)

(25-45 bpm)

N-02

Largo

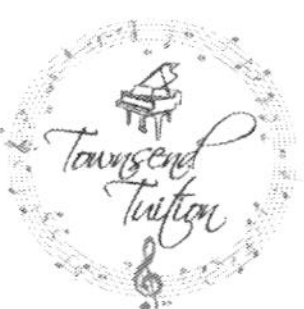

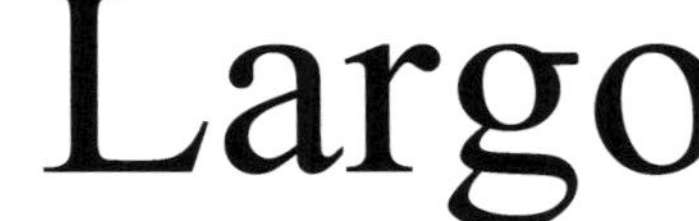

N-03

Townsend Tuition

Slowly (broadly)

(40-60 bpm)

N-03

Lento

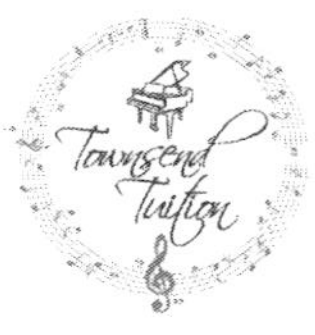

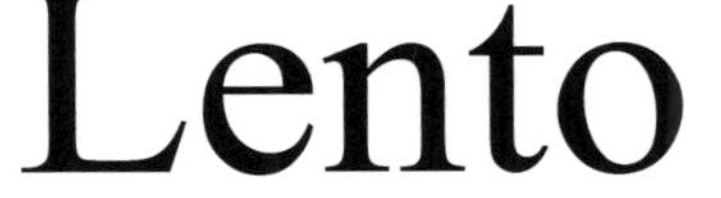

N-04

Slowly

(45-60 bpm)

N-04

Larghetto

N-05

Fairly slowly (and broadly)

(60-66 bpm)

N-05

Adagio

N-06

Slowly with great expression

(66-76 bpm)

N-06

Adagietto

N-07

Fairly slowly (but slightly faster than Adagio)

(70-80 bpm)

N-07

Andante

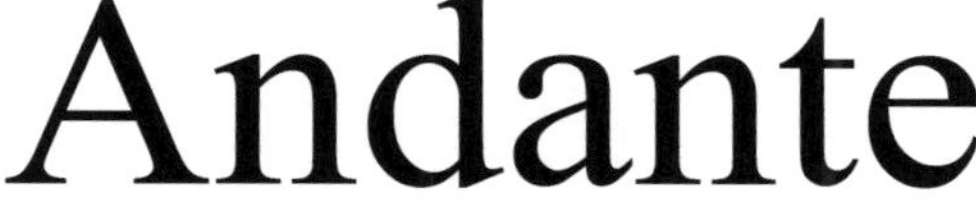

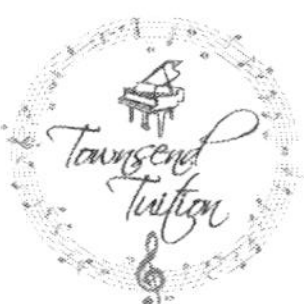

N-08

Walking pace

(78-108 bpm)

N-08

Andantino

N-09

Usually slightly faster than
Andante

(80-108)

N-09

Marcia moderato

N-10

Moderate (in the style of a March)

(83-85 bpm)

N-10

Andante moderato

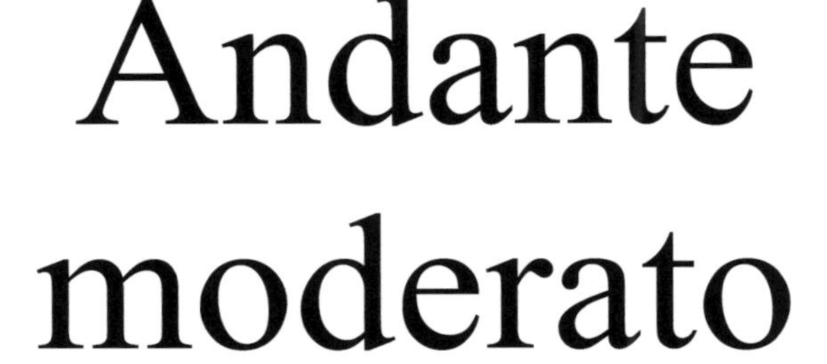

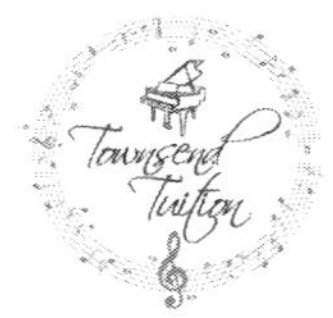

N-11

Between Andante and Moderato

(92-112 bpm)

N-11

Moderato

N-12

At a moderate speed

(108-120 bpm)

N-12

Allegretto

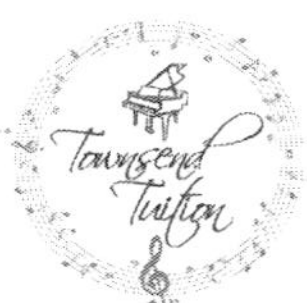

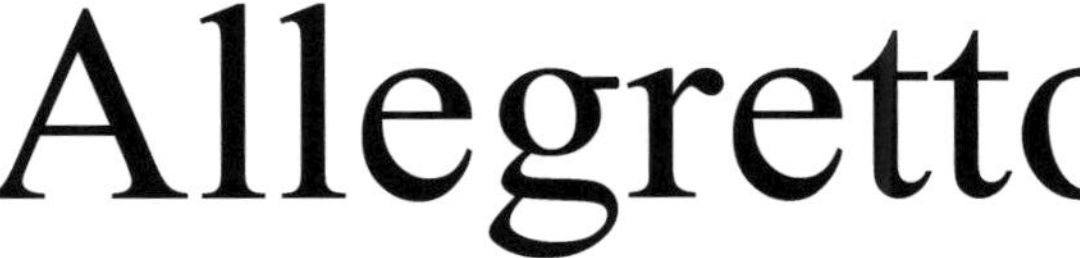

N-13

Moderately fast

(112-120 bpm)

N-13

Allegro moderato

N-14

A little slower than Allegro

(116-120 bpm)

N-14

Allegro

N-15

Quickly and bright

(120-156 bpm)

N-15

Vivace

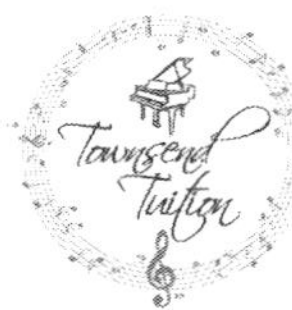

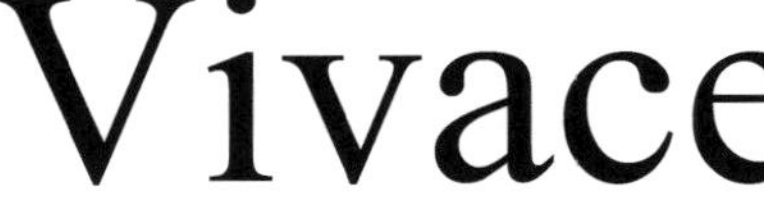

N-16

Lively and fast

(156-176 bpm)

N-16

Vivacissimo

N-17

Very fast and lively

(172-176 bpm)

N-17

Allegrissimo

N-18

Very fast
(Allegro vivace)

(172-176 bpm)

N-18

Allegro vivace

N-19

Very fast
(Allegrissimo)

(172-176 bpm)

N-19

Presto

N-20

Very, very fast

(168-200 bpm)

N-20

Prestissimo

N-21

Even faster than presto

(200 bpm and over)

N-21

a piacere

O-01

At pleasure
(At the performer’s
discretion)

O-01

Townsend
Tuition

con moto

O-02

With movement

e.g. Allegro con moto
(Quickly with movement)

O-02

assai

O-03

Very

e.g. Allegro assai
(Very quickly)

O-03

a tempo

O-04

Resume previous tempo

O-04

l’istesso tempo

O-05

At the same speed
(even when time signature or
note length has changed)

O-05

ma non tanto

O-06

But not so much

e.g. Adagio ma non tanto
(Slow, but not so much)

To a lesser degree than Ma non troppo

O-06

ma non troppo

O-07

But not too much

e.g. Allegro ma non troppo
(Fast, but not too much)

O-07

molto

O-08

Very

e.g. Molto allegro
(Very quickly)

O-08

poco

O-09

A little

e.g. Accelerando poco a poco
(Getting faster little by little)

O-09

subito

O-10

Suddenly

e.g. subito forte
(suddenly loud)

O-10

tempo comodo

O-11

At a comfortable speed

O-11

tempo di

O-12

Speed of a…

e.g. Tempo di valzer

(Speed of a waltz: ♩. = 60 bpm)

Tempo di marcia

(Speed of a march: ♩ = 120 bpm)

O-12

tempo guisto

O-13

In exact time

O-13

tempo
semplice

O-14

Simple, regular speed

O-14

tempo primo

O-15

Resume original (first) tempo

O-15

Accelerando

P-01

Gradually speeding up

P-01

P-02

Gradually speeding up

(Accelerando)

P-02

P-03

Decreasing tempo

P-03

P-04

Going slower

(And usually also softer)

P-04

Doppio movimento

P-05

Double speed

P-05

Doppio più lento

P-06

Half speed

P-06

Lentando

P-07

Gradually slowing

(And usually also softer)

P-07

Meno mosso

P-08

Less quickly

P-08

Piú mosso

P-09

More quickly

P-09

Mosso

P-10

Quicker

(Not as much as Piú mosso)

P-10

Precipitando

P-11

Going faster

P-11

Rallentando

P-12

Gradually slowing down

P-12

P-13

Gradually slowing down

(Rallentando)

P-13

Ritardando

P-14

Slowing down gradually

P-14

rit.

P-15

Slowing down gradually

(Ritardando)

P-15

Ritenuto

P-16

Slightly slower

(More immediate and temporary than rall. and rit.)

P-16

riten.

P-17

Slightly slower

(Ritenuto)

(More immediate and
temporary than rall. and rit.)

P-17

Rubato

P-18

Free movement of tempo for expression

P-18

P-19

In a faster tempo

(often near the end of a section)

P-19

Stringendo

P-20

Section gradually increasing in tempo

P-20

Tardando

P-21

Slowing down gradually

(Same as ritardando)

P-21

Printed in Great
Britain
by Amazon